ALISON UTTLEY'S
COUNTRY WALKS
four walks round
Dethick, Lea and Holloway

Freda Bayles
&
Janet Ede
1995

"A five-barred gate is a thing of beauty......a symbol
of safety and home, or of freedom and escape."

Secret Places

CONTENTS

Car Parking

There is a limited amount of road parking in Lea Bridge, Lea and Holloway but roads are narrow, and visitors are asked not to obstruct gateways or access to property.

Car Parks

High Peak Junction on the Cromford-Crich road.

Lea Car Park and Picnic Area, in Lea village on left past Lea Hall.

Wheelchair Access

Walk A - The start of the walk at Lea Bridge.

Walk B - All of this walk which is on roads and pavements although some parts are uphill. Omit woodland section.

Walk C - The start of this walk is in Lea village. Omit woodland footpath and go to Dethick by Shaw Lane, opposite Lea Hall.

Walk D - The Lea Wharf area, but approached by the alleyway off the main road to the Hat Factory, see D 11.

Toilets

High Peak Junction Workshops - cross by bridge from car park.

Church Street, Holloway.

Disabled toilets at Arkwright's Mill and Cromford Market Place.

Transport to the area

Lea and Holloway can be reached by train from Derby and Matlock, alighting at Cromford for Lea Bridge, about a mile's walk on a busy road. An alternative walk is along the Cromford Canal towpath to High Peak Junction and Lea Bridge. From Whatstandwell station there is a steady uphill walk of about a mile and a quarter to Holloway. Outside the station turn right and right again before the pub, then take the lane signed for Holloway.

Bus services are available from Chesterfield, Manchester, Nottingham, Buxton and Derby. For timetable see useful telephone numbers, page 5.

As a child Alison Uttley visited a number of places in the district, which may be reached by car or other transport. They are often disguised with different names, as river Darrant for Derwent, but it is possible to recognise her references to Cromford and Wirksworth, see *Our Village*, the Matlocks and Bakewell where she went by train to school. The ruined Wingfield Manor, important to *The Traveller in Time*, can be seen from the Crich-Alfreton road; it is rarely open to the public .

Useful telephone numbers.

Local bus and train timetables plus much useful information are available in "Peak District Timetable" price 50p. published by Derbyshire County Council Transport Unit, obtainable from Council Offices and many retail outlets.

Derbyshire County Council 01629 580000

Derbyshire Dales District Council 01629 580580

Tourist Information centre, Matlock Bath 01629 55082

Tourist Information Centre, Bakewell 01629 813227

Arkwright's Mill, Cromford 01629 824297

High Peak Junction Information Centre 01629 822831

Matlock Library, Steep Turnpike, Matlock 01629 582480
- small local history collection.

Derbyshire Record Office, Ernest Bailey Buildings, New Street, Matlock 01629 580000 Ex. 7347
- County collection of archive material and maps.

Local Studies Library, County Offices, Bank Road, Matlock 01629 580000 Ex 6597.
- an extensive collection of printed materials, old newspapers, Census records and St. Catherine's House Indexes.

ACKNOWLEDGEMENTS

Thanks are due to George Wigglesworth, Angus and Merren Watson for their helpful comments on the manuscript, to Mrs Clay for the loan of photographs, to Scarthin Books for the cover illustration and to Derek Peck and Alan Dare for help with illustrations and maps.

Thanks are also due to the friends who have walked with us - Jean Eyre, Ann Coates, Mark Sherin, and Kim, whose four paws have covered all the ground.

Alison Uttley in her garden at Thackers, with Macduff.

Alison Uttley - Her early life

Castle Top Farm, even today, is only reached by a steep track rising from the Lea road. Here Alice Jane Taylor, later to be known as Alison Uttley, was born on 17th December, 1884, the first child of Henry Taylor and his wife Hannah. In keeping with the country tradition she was warmly wrapped and carried up to the attic, for a new born child had to go up before being taken downstairs, so that it would always rise in the world. There had been a snowstorm, and she described "being held up to the windows to open my eyes and to look out over the fields at the dazzling whiteness." *A Peck of Gold*

This snow baby was surely destined to rise in the world, to become a storyteller with a magical quality. In later years she created Little Grey Rabbit, Brock the Badger, Mouldy Warp, Sam Pig and other animal characters loved by generations of children. Her many adult works, especially *The Country Child* are sharply evocative of Derbyshire rural life of a century ago, a harder yet possibly a happier time than we know today.

Farming was hard and precarious work in this rugged hill country. Her family were tenant farmers, as they had been for some two hundred years at Castle Top and there never was much money to spare. Yet there was a basic security in the close agricultural community. She recalled how snug they felt on winter nights, knowing that their animals were safe in the barns, and the family cosy beside the kitchen fire, with shutters and curtains drawn to keep out the cold and the storm.

The farm had abundant water supplies from springs and a well, and was self sufficient as Henry Taylor was a good farmer. Hannah Taylor had been a lady's maid before marriage, and brought some refinement to the home. Old brass candlesticks were kept well polished and oil lamps kept trimmed; fine sewing was done on winter nights as well as rag rugs and patchwork quilts being made. The dairy was kept spotless; surplus food was always preserved and bread was made at home.

Until a younger brother came along there were no playmates nearby, and Alison made friends of the animals, the trees and flowers, even the stones on the farm. She was intensely aware of everything around her, noting the smoothness of pebbles, fossils in the limestone walls, and the delicate structure of ferns growing in the water trough. Castle Top was her whole world in those early years, and later she could recall and describe minutely and beautifully every facet of her surroundings, every activity carried out by her parents and the farm servants, both outside and inside.

The family loved their home, with wide views over the Derwent river to Cromford and beyond, with the sheltering hills behind. As they grew up the children could venture further from the farm and discover new pathways and tracks, and enjoy visits to neighbours and friends in the surrounding farms and villages.

Lea, Holloway and Dethick, a brief history and introduction.

The four walks which follow have been planned to introduce the visitor to places familiar to Alison Uttley as she grew up at Castle Top Farm, and to indicate briefly how the sights and memories of childhood played an important part in her writing.

From her home she could glimpse Cromford and Wirksworth, the small market communities she visited with her father in their pony and trap. Equally familiar were the four small hamlets of Lea Bridge, Holloway, Lea and Dethick in the parish of Ashover; these became her wider world when she started school.

A turning off the A6 at Cromford takes the visitor along the Crich road to Lea Bridge, the starting point for three of the walks. Here the ancient trackway from Cromford Bridge crossed Lea Brook before the lower turnpike road was built in the 1780's. This path clung to the hillside below Castle Top Farm, providing an alternative route to the easily flooded valley bottom road.

From the Lea Bridge crossing the road ran sharply up to Crich and beyond, passing through Holloway. (A `hollow way' was the name used to describe a way deepened by regular passage of pack ponies and travellers).

Lead and water helped to shape the landscape and the lives of the villagers. Lea Brook, a narrow but fast flowing stream, runs under the road at Lea Bridge, fed from the moors above Dethick and Riber. Its energy supplied the power for a number of corn mills, water-powered bellows to heat the lead smelting furnaces, Lea Mills textiles and the Hat Factory at Lea Wharf.

Just as Richard Arkwright had harnessed the power of Bonsall Brook and Cromford Sough for his cotton mills at Cromford, so the Nightingales used water to develop industry in Lea. They were a local family, owning extensive tracts of land in Derbyshire, with valuable mineral and lead smelting rights. Peter Nightingale II (1736-1803) built Lea Mills in 1784, originally for the spinning of cotton, but later leased it to the Smedley family who changed production to wool in 1818.

The long history of the mill can be seen in its varied building styles, ranging from stone cottages on the left (now derelict) with graded stone roofing, to the later redbrick buildings of the 1920's and 30's. Many date plaques incorporated into the buildings are visible from the road.

Peter Nightingale II was also responsible for developing the canal arm from Lea Bridge which made it easier to transport lead ingots and textiles to the main Cromford canal and beyond.

He died in 1803 leaving his fortune to his nephew, William, who together with his daughter, Florence Nightingale, became a benefactor to the village.

The Smedleys, too, contributed to the wealth and life of Lea and Holloway, developing housing for their workers, medical facilities at Post Office Row, a Methodist Chapel, and in more recent times Lea Rhododendron Gardens. John Smedley was later to pioneer hydropathic treatment in Matlock, and to build Riber Castle.

Mining and smelting of lead was an ancient industry which had drawn the Romans to Derbyshire. Wood from the hillsides, and later water, provided power for smelting and helped make the fortunes of the Babingtons of Dethick, of Peter Nightingale and later the Wass family. They owned Mill Close mine at Darley Dale, one of the last commercial lead mines in the country. Their ore was brought by carts to the smelter by the stream above Lea Mills. The flames from its furnace were seen by Alison on her way to school.

Alison would have known Lea Bridge as a busy industrial settlement, with workers coming to Lea Mills from as far away as Clay Cross. The hum of mill machinery, the sound of the mill hooter marking the start and finish of each day would have been part of her life, as was the sight of workers taking their breaks outside the factory, smoking their clay pipes. Carts carrying lead ore and ingots pulled up the inclines, while milk and farm produce rattled down the hillsides to feed the nearby farms and villages.

We hope this short introduction to Alison Uttley's early life will help the visitor to enjoy these four walks as well as the reading of her books.

Broad-leaved Garlic

Walk A

Park in the vicinity of Lea Bridge or at High Peak Junction Car Park.

On this walk we trace Alison's steps between Castle Top Farm and Lea Bridge, a walk she made each day to school. We can return by the same route, or continue past the farm, enjoying spectacular views over Cromford, Matlock Bath, Holloway and Crich, before dropping down into Lea village and returning to Lea Bridge.

A1.   At Lea Bridge pass through the stile to the left of the motor workshop, ignoring the Splash Farm sign to the right. Climb up through Bow Wood which is largely deciduous, of sturdy oak, birch and beech, with plantations of fir and larch. Trees of this ancient coppiced woodland provided fuel for the local lead smelters. This track formed part of the old road from Cromford to Crich as the valley bottom was liable to flooding, before the building of the turnpike in the late 18th century.

In Alison's day this was a wide track which could take a coal dray from Lea Wharf. An elderly resident describes how it rocked and jolted as the horses picked their way over large boulders. In the lamplight he could see the clusters of empty hazelnuts left by squirrels on the tops of walls. *Reminiscences IV.*

A2.   Pause some 50 yards beyond the Woodland Trust board on your right and look down through the clearing. Here the panorama is largely unchanged from Alison's day. Below lie the River Derwent, the Cromford Canal, High Peak Junction workshops, the railway line, the tall chimney of Leawood Pumphouse, and the highroad (A6) beyond. On the far side is a high retaining wall which crosses the fields, part of the High Peak Railway from the Manchester area to Cromford. Above lie wooded slopes and the expanse of Cromford Moor.

A3.   Continue to climb through birch woodland with millstone grit walls on the right. Alison loved the variety of trees on the hillsides around the farm. The beeches with smooth grey trunks and huge, twisted knobbly roots formed seats and hiding places for secret treasures. In autumn they flamed like fire; in spring they were "delicately coloured as clouds." Nothing grew beneath their canopy. Their branches, low and dipping, barred her pathway, and the looming shapes in the dusk were menacing and threatening on the homeward journey from school. She described herself as Red Riding Hood in her cloak, carrying the lantern she had left hidden on the morning journey, aware of the sharp eyes of woodland creatures watching her. She battled through wind, lost and defenceless, until she reached the safety of the farm, a "Noah's Ark cut off from the drowned black world outside." *The Country Child.*

Bow Wood ".... great crooked individual wayside trees....almost menacing with outstretched arms .... and waving branches."

Secret Places

A4.   At the top of the rise go through the next pinch stile with open fields on the left. The view of Cromford below is one Alison enjoyed in the summer. In her day from a seat under the oaks she could see a patchwork of small fields, and cricketers playing on the meadows below, looking like clockwork toys. By the canal is the square grey shape of Rock

House, (principal home of Richard Arkwright), Dene quarry on the far right, and Bole Hill where now the skyline is crowned by a transmitter. She described the dark, tree-ringed skyline as "circling the cup of the world." *The Country Child.*

A5. Continue past Sunny Bank cottage on the right and cross on to the tarmac track to climb up to Castle Top Farm, almost hidden by the high walls which protect it from the weather. (Visitors are asked to respect the privacy of the property).

This small hillside farm was rented by Alison's family from the Arkwrights, and had been farmed by them for generations. Although the soil was thin and stones stuck through like ribs, her father made a success of his work in this harsh landscape, seeing that the animals were sleek and well-fed. He and Alison's mother were equally caring of their domestic servants and the itinerant Irish labourers who helped with the harvest.

It was this awareness of continuity in life and landscape which helped to shape the writer and sustain her in difficult later years. "Every tree or rock, highroad or footpath seemed to carry a story." *Ambush of Young Days.* These memories are woven into the fabric of all her writing.

The Irishmen's Place, where they stayed while harvesting.

A6. Take the broad path which curves in front of the house. This ancient track, described by Alison as a "green ribbon threading the woods and fields", would once have carried the pony packtrains from the Cromford river crossing to the villages of Lea, Riber and Dethick. *The Country Child.* Alison and her brother knew this as Boggart's Lane, a boggart being a half-human creature. They were always glad to reach the more friendly ground of Bilberry Knoll and Hearthstone Farm where they visited friends on their walk to Riber.

A7. Pass through the pinch stile where from the open view on the left can be seen Willersley Castle, the country house built by Sir Richard Arkwright in 1791. On the right are glimpses of Matlock Bath where the cable cars carry visitors up to the Heights of Abraham and the Victoria Prospect Tower.

"Derbyshire Stiles ....are narrow....to keep a calf from passing through ....wide enough for a slim human being."

Secret Places

A8. Pass through the stone gate posts noting the arrow benchmarks from which the height above sea level can be measured. Walk through the next gate, turning back to note the masts of Alport Heights. Alison loved the walls on this walk, their shapes and colours embroidered with silvery lichens and miniature tree-like mosses and fungi. On these childhood walks we can see the observer and scientist emerging, and realise how her poet's eye and voice would convey a sense of wonder to her readers.

13

A9.   Continue up the hollow trackway into the woodland. At the tall holly hedge on the right note the high wooden stile, directly opposite the small stone pinch stile on the old track up from Cromford Bridge. Climb over the wooden stile into the field, following the yellow waymarks. The path as marked on the OS map has been changed. Work round the edge of the fields bearing right, with the steep drop of Coumbs wood and quarry on the right. Below are views of Holloway, Lea School, the church and, on the left, the square tower of Dethick Church. In the distance on your right is Crich Stand. Immediately below is the large mound of lead-smelting waste which is all that remains of the Lea Smelting Works.

A10.   Drop down the fields following the edge round to the right, until reaching the broad green trackway. Turn right along this track, ignoring the left waymark, and take the small stone stile through the holly wood. Cross the trackway past the rhododendrons and water department buildings, and then take the stile on the left.

A11.   Cross Littlemoor Brook by the ancient stepping stones, and take the stile on to the Riber Road. Go through the next stile directly opposite and climb the field path into Lea village, coming out by the old Moot Hall, once a village Reading Room.

For a direct return to Lea Bridge turn right down the hill and then walk along the main road. On the right is Lea Brook with some small farms near its banks. The Great Dam by Pear Tree Farm powered Smedleys Mill and provided fishing and boating facilities. Smedleys maintained their own horse-drawn fire-engine (an elderly resident has given a graphic account in *Reminiscences IV* of fighting a fire at Pear Tree Farm, using water from the Dam). **For a circular walk join Walk C, page 22.**

Walk B

Park near Lea Bridge or at High Peak Junction Car Park.

This walk continues Alison's school journey from Lea Bridge along Lea road and up the path to Lea School, and offers an optional woodland walk, returning via Crich road to Lea Bridge.

Alison Uttley was taught at home by her mother until seven years old when decisions needed to be made about sending her to school. The farm was a long way from any school but the one at Lea seemed most suitable for it had a fine headmaster, Mr Allen, a scholar, scientist and musician with a reputation for good discipline.

B1.   From the stile at Bow Wood Alison would have walked through Lea Bridge, bearing left towards Smedleys Factory. Standing high on the right is the Post Office, the end one of a row of cottages which had originally been used as a hospital for Smedleys workers. These cottages retain their fine old stone roofing tiles. Pass Smedleys Factory, which now bears a memorial plaque on the wall commemorating the men whose lives were sacrificed in two world wars. On the right under the overhead bridge stood a small cottage which was also a shop selling all manner of goods. It was kept by a formidable lady who was sometimes unwilling to come and serve a child, but Alison occasionally entered bravely to buy sweets.

B2.   Pass the mill reservoir on the left. After 200 yards is a pleasant row of cottages built by John Smedley about 1900 for his workers and bearing a plaque on a wall. 100 yards further on is the site of a former lead works in an area once known as Cowhay. In *Cuckoo in June* Alison described the fiery furnace she sometimes saw alight, and clouds of yellow sulphurous smoke escaping. Working with lead was harmful to the workers and the Manager of the plant was empowered to provide regular milk and fat bacon sandwiches for them, to absorb the dangerous lead dust. *Lead Smelting in Lea.*

Next is a dwelling first called Leadworks Cottage and later known as Snowball Cottage, through being occupied by John Snowball, a mill manager and chapel deacon. His was the last leadworking family to live there.

B3.   After 150 yards turn right onto a walled footpath. This is a delightful ascent from the Lea road to the Holloway road, and comes out within sight of Lea School.

MAP OF CROMFORD, L

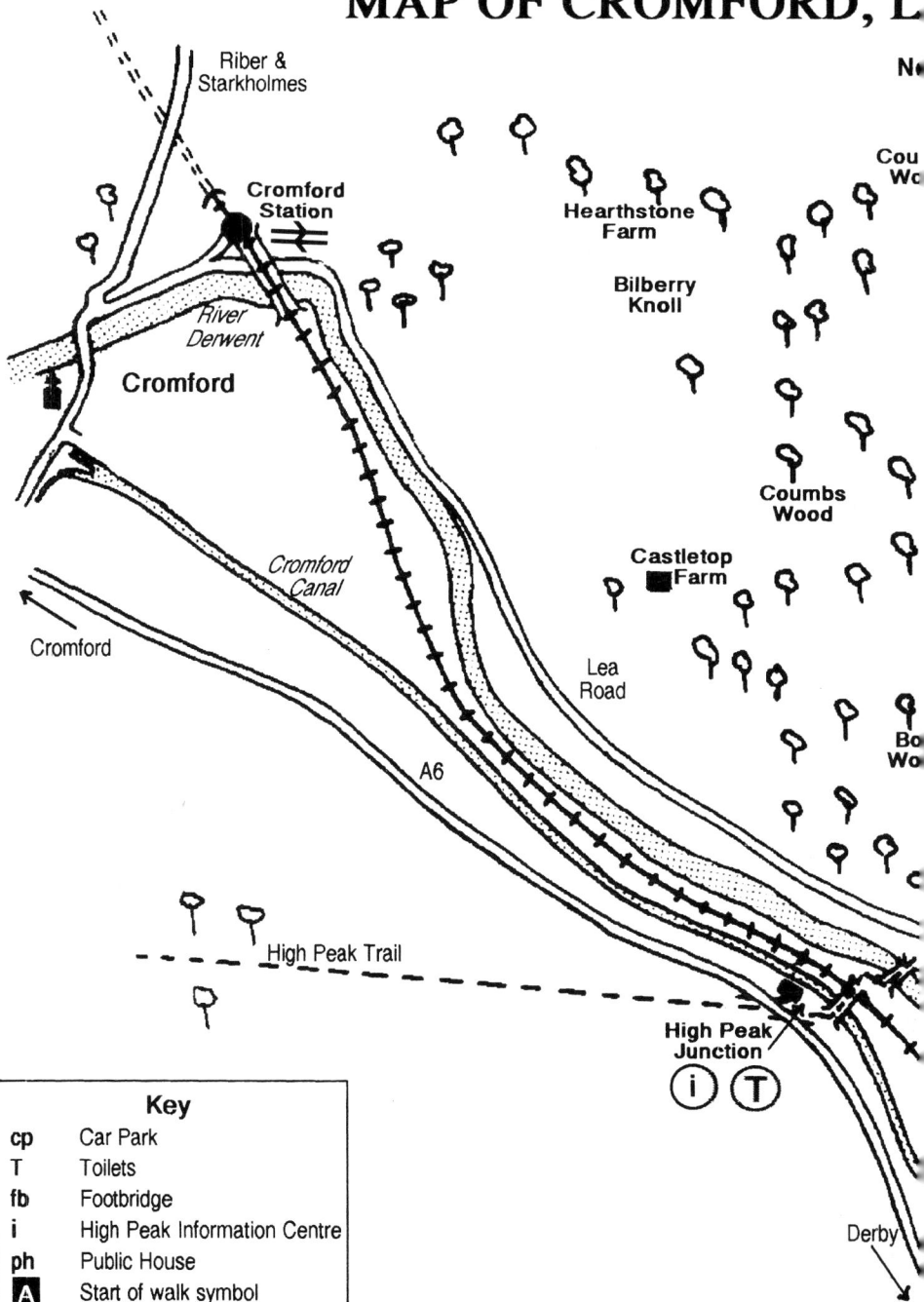

Riber &
Starkholmes

Cromford
Station

Hearthstone
Farm

Cou
Wo

*River
Derwent*

Cromford

Bilberry
Knoll

*Cromford
Canal*

Cromford

Coumbs
Wood

Castletop
Farm

Lea
Road

A6

Bo
Wo

High Peak Trail

High Peak
Junction

(i) (T)

Derby

Key	
cp	Car Park
T	Toilets
fb	Footbridge
i	High Peak Information Centre
ph	Public House
A	Start of walk symbol
Refer to Ordnance Survey	
Outdoor Leisure Map 24.1994	

BRIDGE & HOLLOWAY

Lea

le

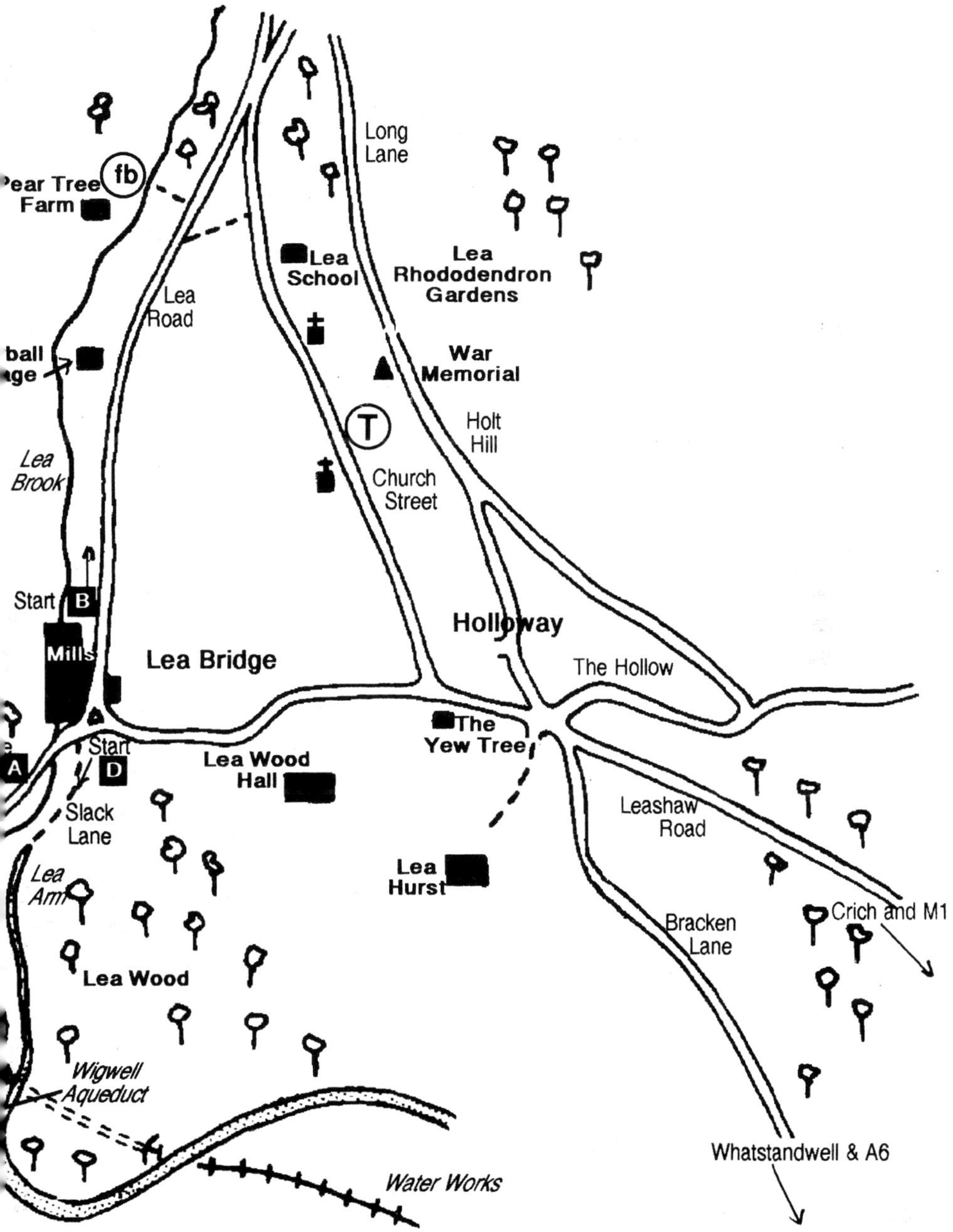

Long Lane
fb
ear Tree Farm
Lea School
Lea Rhododendron Gardens
Lea Road
ball
ge
War Memorial
T
Holt Hill
Lea Brook
Church Street
Start
B
Mills
Holloway
Lea Bridge
The Hollow
The Yew Tree
Start
D
A
Lea Wood Hall
Slack Lane
Leashaw Road
Lea Hurst
Lea Arm
Bracken Lane
Crich and M1
Lea Wood
Wigwell Aqueduct
Whatstandwell & A6
Water Works

Lea School, for the education of a country child.

B4. Some years earlier Alice's father, Henry Taylor, had attended a dame school at Common End. This is now a private house called The Beeches and bears a plaque on the wall. (To see it turn left and make a short diversion). This was superseded by a new school at Holloway about 1859, which continued to be known as Lea School. In 1888 the building was improved, so it would have looked fine when Alison arrived there with her mother and was enrolled on 4th April 1892, under her then name of Alice Jane Taylor.

She had already a good grasp of the 3R's but was placed in the infants' room on that first day, looking an odd little figure in somewhat old fashioned clothing. "When were you born?" asked the teacher. "On a Saturday," she replied. She was given childish tasks to do; threading coloured paper into mats, counting beads on an abacus, and decided it was very boring and she would not attend the school any more, but her mother laughed at her and sent her to school again the next day. This time she dawdled through the woods and arrived very late. In *A 10 O'clock Scholar* she described lifting the latch of the big schoolroom door, entering quietly and standing still while 100 eyes turned to stare at her.

18

She soon settled down at school, found her own level and revelled in learning. Summer attendance would have been a pleasure, with lessons sometimes taken out of doors, but winter was hard. Sometimes she arrived at school very wet, to be undressed, wrapped in a blanket, and dried out before the kitchen fire in the schoolhouse. Because of the long journey she was allowed to take her lunch to school, and to have a hot drink.

The headmaster's wife taught the infant classes, and was sometimes seen hurrying from the classroom through to the schoolhouse, perhaps to check on a meal cooking, or to pick up a crying baby and bring it back into class with her. There were two or three pupil teachers in the school as well as an assistant teacher. Fifty boys and girls would be in the main schoolroom, with three or four lessons being given at the same time. Alison often contrived to listen to another lesson near her, and to imbibe French verbs and geography as well as the subject her own class was learning.

Lea School was the hub of social life for the four hamlets, due partly to the strong personality and gifts of the Head. He produced concerts, and the Messiah, and even once an operetta. Alison has described how every one was drawn into this. Those unable to sing or play an instrument helped with costume and scenery making. Her parents lent fine old brass candlesticks and pewter tankards as stage props, and attended the performance, driving to school in their pony trap dressed in Sunday best clothes.

She gained a very good all round education at the school, studying geology, history, music, science, as well as the 3R's and sewing, which she detested. She would have preferred being with the boys in their gardening class to sitting inside plying a stubborn needle. With only one small brother at home she was a lonely child, so mixing with other children helped overcome some of her shyness. She would tell them tales of the farm and the animals and entice them to walk a short part of the long way home with her "to hear the rest of the story." On dark winter nights she was allowed to leave early, and did the whole long walk back alone. *The Country Child.*

Holloway Church.

B5.   This walk continues past Lea School towards Holloway. On the left, before Christ Church, the parish church built in 1901, is a footpath sign, and it is worth making a detour to go up this delightful woodland path to Holt Hill, a quiet lane from which can be seen Lea Green (now an educational Centre) and Dethick Church tower, and other more distant views. **Turn right, walk about 100 yards passing a footpath sign on the right, go another 100 yards and take the next footpath downhill, through the wicket gate.** Surrounded by rhododendrons and woodland is the War Memorial bearing the names of local men who died in two world wars. From the plinth of the memorial the view is superb. The ruins of Riber Castle dominate the skyline. It was built by John Smedley in 1862 as a family home, and later was used as a school. John Summerson in his book *The Unromantic Castle* describes his days there in the ''gaunt, bare schoolrooms... It compels the attention in that big-boned Derbyshire landscape...... raw and uncouth... not easily forgotten.'' Alison enjoyed walking over the fields to the little hamlet which included Riber Hall and Manor House. Wirksworth and Middleton with their quarries lie ahead; directly below and in front is Smedleys factory chimney.

20

B6.   Walk down through the wood from the War Memorial, a restful descent for there are several seats comfortably placed, and rejoin the Holloway road beside the public toilets. **Continue towards Holloway,** passing some pleasant buildings and the stone Methodist Chapel on the right. This was built in 1852 by John Smedley. Next is the Little London Gallery, originally Nightingale House, one of the Reading Rooms given to the village. At one time newspapers were provided by Florence Nightingale.

B7.   At the grass triangle join the Crich-Cromford road .
The Nightingale Memorial Hall (opened by the Prince of Wales in 1932) stands opposite. **Turn left, uphill,** and walk towards the Yew Tree Inn. Crossing over, note the head of Bracken Lane, which leads down to Whatstandwell. The gates and drive of Lea Hurst, now a retirement home, are on the right. Florence Nightingale, so famous for her fine work during the Crimean War and for her later development of nursing, spent early years living at Lea Hurst with her family. They showed great interest in the village and she retained concern for the schoolchildren throughout her long life. In a chapter on Christmas Cards in her book *Country Things* Alison Uttley recalled how carefully her family treasured the card she had received from Miss Nightingale, by then living quietly in retirement in London.

Walk downhill past the Memorial Hall and back to Lea Bridge, seeing on the right Lea Holme, once owned by the Smedley family, and on the left Lea Wood Hall, which was built for William Walker, owner of the Hat Factory. (see walk D)

For the circular walk join Walk D, page 27.

Walk C

Park in Lea Village near to the crossroads.

C1. At the crossroads look down Baker's Lane opposite Long Lane where there is a house called The Old Moot Hall, which was once a Reading Room for the village. This retains its old stone tiled roof. The entrance to Lea Rhododendron gardens is a short distance up Long Lane. These fine gardens were created by John Marsden Smedley on the site of a former quarry, and are well worth going to see, especially in late spring.

Moot Hall, Lea.

C2. Walk north past Lea Coach House, now an attractive restaurant, and continue through the village.

C3. On the right is the entrance to Lea Green, an educational and sports centre. The house and parkland were formerly owned by the Wass family, who ran the lead smelting works at Lea. They sold it to the Smedley family in 1886, who renovated it in an Elizabethan style.

On the left is the Jug and Glass Inn. The building dates from 1782 and is believed to be on a much older site. Next is a row of nice old cottages bearing the date 1781, which were built by the Nightingale family. **Keep on the road, passing a footpath sign to Dethick and Tansley.**

C4. A Nonconformist chapel stands above the road on the right. There has been a history of worship on this site since the 17th century. Thomas Nightingale, a Unitarian, established a religious meeting place here in

1719. The present building, with three arched windows, is a result of major reconstruction in the 19th century. It incorporates a cottage bearing a date stone of 1671.

Jug and Glass, Lea.

MAP OF LEA & DETHICK

Not to Scale

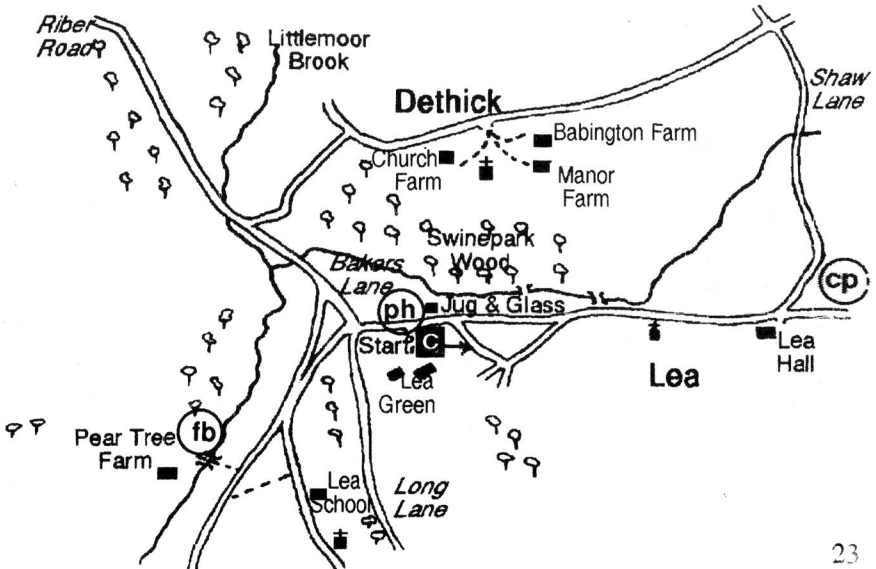

C5.   Continue 50 yards along the road where it is worth looking at Lea Hall, one of the oldest houses in the village. This Manor House has seen some alteration and restoration, including the fine Georgian frontage added by Peter Nightingale in 1754. Perhaps this is the Hall Alison Uttley had in her mind when writing of going out to tea in her book *Secret Places.* She enjoyed the home-cured ham and a sherry trifle, but more important to her was to be in the company of the dignified elderly people whose home this was - "it seemed to be in another century."

Always she had a strong sense of the history of places, and in later years could almost see re-enacted the events of long ago.

C6.   Return along the road to the footpath opposite the chapel, signed Tansley. This goes through Swinepark Wood, crossing Lea Brook by a small stone packhorse bridge and skirting a sloping field. Ahead one can see the tower of Dethick church. The first small stone church dates from the thirteenth century; it was built by Sir Geoffrey Dethick as a small private chapel and dedicated to St John the Baptist. A later Lord of the Manor, Thomas Babington, fought at Agincourt and his son John was killed at Bosworth. A descendant, Sir Anthony Babington, restored the church and added the present tower in 1530.

Lea Hall.

Descriptive leaflets are available in the church, which is open for service on the first Sunday of each month; at other times the key may be obtained from Manor Farm. From the churchyard the view is superb, taking in Riber, woodland, several hamlets and Alport Heights. The hamlet of Dethick (which may be a corruption of Death Oak, a hanging place) is comprised chiefly of three farms, Church Farm, Babington Farm and Manor Farm. This last is built on the site of the old Elizabthan Manor House and the stonework incorporates some of the ruins, including the huge old kitchen.

Alison Uttley was taken to visit Manor Farm several times. Perhaps she walked the path we have used, or came in the pony and trap with her parents. In an age when children were seen and not heard she would have sat quietly while elders talked, but she had a powerful imagination, and the strong atmosphere of the house took hold of her. All her life she experienced vivid dreams which were later recalled and often written down. *The Stuff of Dreams.* She could be in a place and become very aware of times which were past and feel herself to be part of happenings which were long ago. And much had happened long ago at Manor Farm, for these stones were part of the house occupied in the late sixteenth century by the Babington family.

Manor Farm, Dethick.

Anthony Babington was deeply involved in a plot to release Mary Queen of Scots from her imprisonment at Wingfield Manor, some four miles away. There was believed to be an old lead miners' tunnel from Wingfield to Dethick, and it was hoped that this might be used in the escape.

There was also treachery. The plot was discovered and Anthony Babington was executed. Queen Elizabeth stayed safely on her throne and later Queen Mary was beheaded.

Sitting in the old kitchen, Alison was absorbed by the history. Walking about the farms she could see reminders of times past, including an old sixteenth century barn belonging to Church Farm. The Babington Arms can be seen on the wall, as well as on the church tower. Years later she recalled her childhood impressions and wrote *A Traveller in Time*, an historical novel to rank with the very best.

Leave the churchyard by the corner stile, walk down towards the fence and woodland until reaching a footpath sign and a stile. Take the steep stepped track which crosses the Lea Brook by a small packhorse bridge and comes out on to the road. Turn right for Lea village.

For the circular walk go downhill through the village, along the main road and continue to The Beeches at Common End, then join Walk B4 page 15.

Dethick Church

Walk D

Park in the vicinity of Lea Bridge or at the High Peak Junction Car Park.

Beginning at Lea Bridge this walk leads to the wharf area and towpath of the Lea arm of Cromford canal, a favourite walk of Alison's. It was "a private heaven, and the walk beside it a stroll through the gardens of paradise." *Our Village.* The return is via the magnificent Wigwell Aqueduct over the Derwent, High Peak Junction and through the peaceful hamlet of Lea Wood.

D1.   Take the footpath known as Slack Lane on the left of Smedleys Car Park entrance, passing on the left one of the lodges to Lea Hurst, Florence Nightingale's home. This path which leads to Lea Wharf was described at the beginning of the century as "a deeply rutted churned up mess of a road," but littered with what used to be regarded as black treasure - the lumps of coal spilt from carts leaving the wharf and eagerly gathered by local children.

D2.   Pass between the stone pillars which mark the entrance to the wharf area. The silted, overgrown ditch on the left is the dried up arm of Lea Canal, built by Peter Nightingale II in 1800, using water from Lea Brook, and designed to serve the needs of a busy industrial community - the lead works, Lea Mill textiles and the Hat Factory. The arm formed a link with Cromford Canal, opened in 1793, providing access to the Erewash canal.

D3.   It is difficult now to imagine the wharf as the hive of activity it was in Alison's day. The local Co-op barge was one of the brightly painted boats moored there. Coal was brought in from Hartshay near Ripley for Lea Mill Gas Plant, which also provided energy for local houses, including Lea Green. Lead ingots from the Lea Mills smelting works lay here in "silvery piles", waiting to be loaded. The working life of this backwater ended with the closure of the Lea Arm in 1936.

An interesting feature on the wharf is the circular iron base of the old crane used for loading goods from the barges. A weighbridge, now no longer visible, stood between the towpath and Wharf Cottage. **Walk along the towpath passing a tumbledown building** once used for stabling the barge horses.

D4.   Walks along the towpath prompted some of Alison's most evocative writing. Here in high summer, "under the arching tunnel of green gloom", it is possible to sense the contentment and peace she experienced with the reflections and sparkling lights from the canal and river. The canal curves round with Lea Hurst Park on its left and glimpses of the River Derwent on its right.

D5. **Continue along the towpath.** Cross the railway by a footbridge, though the canal would have been carried by an aqueduct. All that remains of this are the projecting buttresses in front of the tunnel walls.

Aqueduct & Cottage

D6. **Walk on to where the Lea Arm joined the main canal.**
Here stands Aqueduct Cottage, described by Alison as "a Hans Anderson dwelling", the place where the fairy tale world of the canal walk and the world of work met. *Our Village.* This ruin was still inhabited in 1919, although primitive. The old lady living there was grateful for lumps of coal thrown by bargees into her small front garden.

Alison loved to lie on the bank of the canal, staring at the myriad, mysterious life in its clear depths - water boatmen, sticklebacks, minnows, tadpoles and small fish; dragonflies and unusual butterflies flew among the massed flowers on the banks. Her eyes close to the surface of the water, she could examine the creatures which skimmed past her nose - "water spiders, carrying silvery bubbles of air ... newts and tiny fish." *Our Village.* From these early enchantments it is possible to see how Alison became interested in science.

D7. **Turn right along Wigwell Aqueduct,** built 1793 by William Jessop to carry Cromford canal over the River Derwent. The tall chimney of Lea Wood pump engine rises above the embankment. This was built in 1849 to draw up water from the Derwent when the canal level was low. For a detailed account of the building of Cromford Canal see *The Cromford Guide.*

Wigwell Aqueduct on the Cromford Canal.

D8. On the opposite bank is the wharf shed, now a Derbyshire County Council Youth Centre, where trucks from the High Peak railway unloaded onto the barges.

D9.Continue to the High Peak Junction workshops, now housing an exhibition, shop and toilets. For a history of the canal and railway see information boards.

D10. **Turn right at the swing bridge,** along the footpath marked Holloway, which winds through the Sewage Works to the High Peak Junction car park.

D11.   Walk out onto the road and turn right, with Bow Wood End on the left. **Turn right down the pathway, between Lea Wood house and Lea Wood cottage;** ahead on the left, on the walls of Brook cottage, are the high projecting stone buttress and iron fittings which are all that remain of the gates to the Hat Factory, built by Peter Nightingale in 1792 and leased out to Lancashire entrepreneurs.

D12.   Turn back and take the footpath by Lea Brook, alongside the high boundary walls of the factory. During its most productive period the factory was run by the Walkers, who built Lea Wood Hall in the 1870's. Military and fashion hats were made here from animal fur and cloth waste. The Peninsular War (1808-1814) and later the Crimean War (1856) created a demand for such hats, but by 1872 the process had become mechanised and production here had ceased. Splashes of blue dye used in the manufacture can still be seen on the wall of the alleyway. Subsequently the building was converted for other uses, but Alison would have known it as a mineral water bottling plant using water from Lea Wood spring, and run by a local family called Else. A Mrs Else kept a small sweet shop on the site, which Alison may have known. Hat Factory Row, facing Lea Wood meadow but now demolished, housed the workers. *Childhood Reminiscences III.* The building became dangerous and in 1955 was demolished, the stone being carted away to build Bow Wood End. Elderly residents in the area have happy memories of the spacious rooms of the factory being used for balls and dances at the turn of the century. **On the wharf turn left for the return to Lea Bridge.**

Alison Uttley described herself after a similar walk as, "a returned traveller, who had seen another world of beauty and tranquillity." *Our Village.* Happy memories remained with her in later life as she sat amidst the painted canal furniture in her kitchen at Penn - a stool with a castle on a hill and a bucket with a wreath of roses on a green background.

Alison Uttley - the later years

At thirteen Alison Uttley gained a scholarship place at Lady Manners School in Bakewell and a wider world began to open for her. She has left vivid descriptions of rising very early to ride down to Cromford Station in the farm cart with the milk.

"I had to remember that I was of less importance than a churn of milk, and if I were only a minute late I should be left behind to run all the way to the station". *Cuckoo in June.*

As had happened at Lea School, she seemed at first an odd little country child to the other pupils, but soon settled down and began to revel in learning. Lessons enchanted her, Latin and music and maths, in which she excelled. One year she won an English prize. She was good at sport and played cricket for the school. Peace and room to study were sometimes hard to find, she has described struggling to get and hold a corner of the kitchen table on which to do her homework. Everyone wanted to use the kitchen table at night. While waiting for the train home in the evening with other pupils, she was pleased to be able to do some homework by the blazing fire in the waiting room at Bakewell Station.

She worked hard and did well throughout her six years at Lady Manners, and in 1903 was awarded a Major County Scholarship for Manchester University.

Now she had to adjust to a much wider world, to leave home and live in a residential college. At first her laundry was sent home, and she loved to get it back, with "a delicious smell of herbs, and flowers and grass" bringing the farm quickly into her mind. Friendships were formed at University; one was with Gertrude Uttley whose brother James would later become Alison's husband.

She loved music, had played the piano from an early age, and now she was able to enjoy concerts, particularly those given by the Hallé Orchestra in Manchester's Free Trade Hall. Literature she still enjoyed, and she contributed to the student magazine, but science was her absorbing interest and her aim was to gain an Honours Degree in Physics. This was accomplished, and in 1907 came another step towards the widening of her world, acceptance at Cambridge to study for a Certificate of Teaching.

At Cambridge a weekly essay was required and she was to recall later "This was the first time in my life I had any good tuition in the art of writing." She was delighted with the beauty of the city, describing the bridges over the river as "poems in stone." From Cambridge she obtained her first teaching appointment, as Junior Science Mistress at a secondary school in Fulham. At first she lodged in Wimbledon and enjoyed walking on the Common "to keep a memory of the country in my mind."

Concerts, theatres, art galleries and museums, all the rich full life of the capital was hers to savour with a number of new friends. This was a time of enjoyment.

Following an engagement of several years, Alison Taylor and James Uttley were married in London in 1911. A scientist and engineer, his work, and his family, were centred in Manchester and he and his bride made their home in Cheshire. Their only child, John Taylor Uttley, was born in 1914. There were visits to Castle Top Farm *(John at the Old Farm* was probably based by Alison on her son's pleasure in staying at his mother's early home) but never for long periods. Her country roots "my background wherever I went" stayed strong in her affection. She had always been a storyteller and now there was a ready audience in her young son. She could remember how large plants and stones and little animals seemed to a small child, and make stories about them. When he went away to boarding school she would write these tales out and send them to him, so Little Grey Rabbit and other characters came into being. She began to write a reminiscence of her childhood. This book, sadly, her husband dismissed as "too childish" yet it recreates, lovingly, the old farm and the people and villages which were the background of her life.

James Uttley died suddenly in 1930, leaving widow and son not too well provided for. With school fees and other demands to be met, Alison began to write with the intention of seeking publication.

The reminiscence was published in 1931 as *The Country Child* and got a warm reception from the public. Her children's stories (about 100 titles) became, and remain, a real pleasure for young people to enjoy. She wrote for magazines and radio and created about 20 adult books, weaving words into magic for some 30 years. From 1938 she lived in Buckinghamshire, generally alone after her son's marriage, in a house called Thackers, the name given to the manor house featured in *A Traveller in Time.* Succeeding Scotch terriers gave her companionship; one, Macduff, was the subject of a book written in 1950. Her long life ended in 1976. She is buried in Penn churchyard, where her grave has the fitting epitaph

"Alison Uttley, writer, a spinner of tales."